HBJ Reading Program

Margaret Early

Bernice E. Cullinan
Roger C. Farr
W. Dorsey Hammond
Nancy Santeusanio
Dorothy S. Strickland

LEVEL 4

Wishes

HBJ **HARCOURT BRACE JOVANOVICH, PUBLISHERS**
Orlando   San Diego   Chicago   Dallas

Acknowledgments

For permission to reprint copyrighted material, grateful acknowledgment is made to the following sources:

Edith Battles: From *Eddie Couldn't Find the Elephants* by Edith Battles. Text © 1974 by Edith Battles.
Crown Publishers, Inc.: Adapted from *Two Hoots and the King* by Helen Cresswell. Copyright © 1977 by Helen Cresswell.
Grosset & Dunlap, Inc.: Adapted from *Mr. Pine's Storybook* (Titled: "Mr. Pine's Town"), written and illustrated by Leonard Kessler. Coyright © 1982 by Leonard Kessler.
Harcourt Brace Jovanovich, Inc.: Adapted from *The Little Red Lighthouse and the Great Gray Bridge* (Titled: "The Little Red Lighthouse") by Hildegarde H. Swift. Copyright 1942 by Harcourt Brace Jovanovich, Inc.; renewed 1970 by Hildegard Hoyt Swift and Lynn Ward.
Harper & Row, Publishers, Inc.: Text and illustrations from "Clouds" in *Mouse Tales*, written and illustrated by Arnold Lobel. Copyright © 1962 by Arnold Lobel. "A Wish is Quite a Tiny Thing" from *FOR DAYS AND DAYS: A Year-Round Treasury of Child Verse* by Annette Wynne. Copyright 1919 by Harper & Row, Publishers, Inc.; renewed 1947 by Annette Wynne. Published by J. B. Lippincott.
Highlights for Children, Inc., Columbus, OH: "The Yellow Monster" by Joanna Cargill in *Highlights for Children*, February 1967. Copyright © 1967 by Highlights for Children, Inc.
Lothrop, Lee & Shepard Books, a division of William Morrow & Company, Inc.: Adapted from *Little Bear Marches in the St. Patrick's Day Parade* (Titled: "The Special Umbrella") by Janice. Copyright © 1967 by Lothrop, Lee & Shepard Co., Inc.
Karen S. Solomon: "How Wise is an Owl" by Ilo Orleans from *The Zoo That Grew*. Published by Henry Z. Walck, Inc.
Franklin Watts, Inc.: Adapted from *Come! Sit! Stay!* by Joan M. Lexau. Text copyright © 1984 by Joan M. Lexau.

Key: (l) – Left; (r) – Right; (c) – Center; (t) – Top; (b) – Bottom

Photographs

Cover: HBJ Photo/John Petrey

Page 2–3, Ewing Galloway; 10, Henry Deters/Monkmeyer Press Photo Service; 11, Carl Centineo/DPI; 12, Taurus Photos; 13, Robert Isear/Photo Researchers; 37, Ewing Galloway; 38(t), NASA from H. Armstrong Roberts, Inc.; 38(cl), Jeffrey Myers/FPG; 38(cr) HBJ Photo; 38(b), H. Armstrong Roberts, Inc.; 39, NASA; 70, August Upitis/Shostal Associates; 71(t), Gail Greig/Shostal Associates; 71(b), Frances Bannett/DPI; 72(t), Leonard Lee Rue, III; 72(b), Robert Ashworth/Photo Researchers; 73(l), Index Stock International; 73(r), Henry Monroe/DPI; 75, NASA; 76, HBJ Photo/Beverly Brosius; 77, HBJ Photo/Beverly Brosius; 104–105, Coco McCoy/Rainbow; 106, HBJ Photo/John Bateman; 107, HBJ Photo/John Bateman; 108, HBJ Photo/John Bateman; 109, HBJ Photo/John Bateman; 113, HBJ Photo/Beverly Brosius; 114–115, E. Streichan/T.P.S.; 134(l), Grant Heilman; 134(r), HBJ Photo; 135(tl), HBJ Photo/Beverly Brosius; 135(bl), HBJ Photo/Beverly Brosius; 135(tr), HBJ Photo/Beverly Brosius; 135(br), HBJ Photo/John Bateman; 136(tl), Paul Conklin/Monkmeyer Press Photo Service; 136(bl), Dan McCoy/Rainbow; 136(tr), Paul Conklin/Monkmeyer Press Photo Service; 136(br), Dan McCoy/Rainbow; 137(tl), Mark Antman/Image Works; 137(bl), HBJ Photo/Beverly Brosius; 137(tr), Mark Antman/Image Works; 137(br), Em Ahart; 138(l), HBJ Photo; 138(r), Tom Meyers; 139(t), Kathruyn Muus; 139(c), HBJ Photo/Beverly Brosius; 139(b) Art Attack; 173, E. Streichan/T.P.S.
Contents: Unit 1, 2–3, Ewing Galloway; Unit 2, 38, HBJ Photo; Unit 3, 76, HBJ Photo/Beverly Brosius; Unit 4, 114–115, E. Streichan/P.P.S.

Illustrators

Terry Anderson: pp. 78–85; Ellen Appleby: pp. 110–111; Gwen Connelly: pp. 4–9, 116–125; Eulala Conner: pp. 14–21, 60–69; Dee Deloy: pp. 86–87; Ethel Gold: pp. 28–33; Leonard Kessler: pp. 126–133; Arnold Lobel: pp. 162–171; Monica Loomis: pp. 34–35; Ben Mahan : pp. 142–151; Mary McLaren: pp. 174–183; Yoshi Miyake: pp. 50–57, 152–153; Jim Noble: pp. 58–59; Bill Ogden: pp. 154–163; Joyce Orchard: pp. 96–103; Jerry Smath: pp. 40–49; Mark Stanton: pp. 88–95; Chip Weston: pp. 140–141; Bernard Wiseman: pp. 22–27.

Printed in the United States of America

ISBN 0-15-330504-5

Contents

Unit 4 Old Days, Old Ways **114**

Wishes

Rainbows

In "Rainbows," you will read stories that have colors in them.

Red, orange, yellow, green, blue, and purple are some of the colors you will be reading about in this unit.

These are the colors of the rainbow, too.

As you read the stories, look for some of these colors.

Look to see why colors are important in the stories.

Some boys and girls go to see a
big yellow monster.
What is the monster?

The Yellow Monster

by Joanna Cargill

Nina ran to Tim's house.

"Come and see a monster,"
Nina said to Tim.
"It is big and yellow.
It is near my house."

"I don't know if I want
to see a monster," said Tim.

"You don't have to be afraid.
You can just watch the monster.
You don't have to get too near it,"
said Nina.

"I will come with you," said Tim.
"Let's get Rick, too."

Nina and Tim ran to get Rick.
"You must see the monster!
It is a big, yellow, helping monster.
It likes to dig.
Come with us, Rick," said Nina.

"I will come with you.
Let's get Linda, too," said Rick.
"She likes to watch monsters."

So Nina, Tim, and Rick ran
to get Linda.

"Linda, you must come and see the
monster near Nina's house.
It is big and yellow," said Tim.

"It digs up things," said Rick.

"It pushes things, too," said Nina.

"Will it push me?" asked Linda.

"It will not push you," said Nina.
"You don't have to be afraid.
You will like to watch it."

So Nina, Tim, Rick, and Linda ran to Nina's house.

"Here is the monster," said Nina. "Don't go too near it."

"Oh, I know what that is," said Linda.

"This monster is big and yellow. It's a helping monster," said Tim.

"It's big and yellow and helping.
But it is not a monster at all,"
said Rick.

Nina, Tim, Rick, and Linda
see that the monster is just
a bulldozer.
Now read to find out what a
bulldozer can do.

The Bulldozer

by Edward D. Mullett

Look at this bulldozer.
It is big, and it is yellow.
A bulldozer can dig.
A bulldozer can push.
It can push many things.
It can push away big rocks.

This bulldozer is pushing.
It is pushing away big rocks.
Soon there will be a new road.
There will be a new school, too.

This bulldozer is digging.
It is digging a big hole.
This big hole is for the new school.

Many girls will come down this
new road.

Many boys will come, too.

They will go to the new school.

Pam and Jan both get new blue bikes.

How will Pam know her bike?

How will Jan know her bike?

Blue Bikes

by Margaret Braden

Pam called Jan and said, "I got a new bike."

Jan said, "I did, too."

"My bike is blue," said Pam.

"So is mine!" said Jan. "I will show it to you at school."

"You can see mine there, too,"
said Pam.

When Pam and Jan got to school,
they looked at the bikes.
"Your bike is just like mine!"
said Pam.

"Our bikes are just the same!
"I'm glad," said Jan.

Pam said, "So am I."

When the girls came out of school, Pam asked Jan, "Is this my bike?"

"These bikes look the same to me," said Jan.

"I want to take my bike home," said Pam.

"I want to take my bike home, too.
Let's think what we can do,"
said Jan.

"My house is on this side
of the school.

So I came from this side.

I put my bike here," said Pam.

"My house is on that side
of the school.

So I came from that side.

I put my bike there," said Jan.

"This blue bike is mine,"
said Pam.

"Then this blue bike must be
mine!" said Jan.

At Pam's house her dad said,
"I got something for your new bike.
   It is a tag with *Pam* on it.
   I will help you put it on your bike."

"Oh, thank you, Dad.
   I need this tag," said Pam.

Pam called Jan and said, "My
dad got something for my
new bike."

Jan said, "My dad got something
for my new bike, too.
I will show it to you at school."

"I will show you what I got, too,"
said Pam.

At school the girls looked at the
tags on the bikes.

"My tag isn't like yours," said Jan.

"Our tags are not the same,"
said Pam.

"I'm glad our bikes are not just
the same now," said Jan.

A big goose shows a little goose a special thing.
What is that special thing?

Little Goose

story and pictures by Bernard Wiseman

22

"Oh, look at that," said the little goose.

"I want to follow the yellow and orange."

"You can't follow the yellow and orange," said the big goose.

"If you follow them, you will get lost."

23

"Oh," said the little goose.
"Look at that duck!
I like purple.
I will follow that purple duck."

"Stop," said the big goose to the little goose.

"You will get lost if you follow the purple duck.

Come down here with me.

Soon you will see yellow and orange.

You will see purple and red, too."

The little goose went flying down to the big goose.

"Where is the yellow and orange? Where is the purple and red?"

"Look there," said the big goose.

"Oh, I like that!" said the little goose.

"That is special."

"Yes, it is," said the big goose.
"Now the sun is going down.
When the sun comes up, it will bring a new day.
Then you can fly up into the blue."

Sequence

Look at the pictures.
They show what comes first,
next, and last to make
a road.

A.

B.

C.

Which picture comes first?
Which picture comes next?
Which picture comes last?

Which picture comes first?
Which picture comes next?
Which picture comes last?

A.

B.

C.

Now read these sentences.

A. Nina comes to Pam's house.

B. Pam wants Nina to come to her house for lunch.

C. Nina and Pam have lunch.

Which sentence comes first?
Which sentence comes next?
Which sentence comes last?

You have read some stories with colors in them. Now read to find out how you can mix colors to make a rainbow.

Paint a Rainbow

by Althea Rahz

Look at a rainbow.
What colors do you see?

Red, yellow, and blue paint
will help you make all the colors
of the rainbow.

1. How are Mr. Fig, Little Feet, and Eddie alike?

   How are they different?

2. Little Feet went to look for a horse that was far away. Where else can you find a horse?

3. Eddie went to the zoo and saw an elephant.

   What other animals can you see at a zoo?

4. Which story did you like best? Why?

Winks and Blinks

Do you know what a wink is?

A wink is one way of telling your feelings.

A wink can tell a friend that you are happy.

Do you know what a blink is?

A blink is one way to show that you are surprised.

Being surprised is a feeling, too.

As you read the stories in "Winks and Blinks," look for some special feelings.

A girl wants to teach her dog to come, sit, and stay. How does the girl do this?

Come! Sit! Stay!

by Joan M. Lexau

Tiny, you are getting big.
I will teach you some things.
I will teach you to come when
I say *come.*

I'll wait here.
Tiny, Tiny. Get over here.
Oh, I forgot.
I have to say *come,* or you
won't know what to do.
Come, Tiny. Come here!

78

That's great! You did it!
Tiny, you are a good dog.
Thank you for coming when
I called.
Let me hug you.

Let's do it again.
Tiny, come! Come to me.
That's a good dog.
How about a big hug?

Now let's play with this ball.

No, Tiny, don't jump on me!
Get off!
I don't like that.
We can't play with this ball.
I'll have to teach you to *sit*.
Then I can make you *sit* when you
want to jump on me.

Sit, Tiny, sit!
That's it. That's a good dog.

Let's see if you can sit again.
Sit, Tiny, sit!
No! No! No!
I didn't say to sit on me.

Get up, Tiny! Get up!

Oh, Tiny, I'm not mad at you.
You did sit.
That's a good dog.

Now I'll teach you to *stay*.
Stay!

Tiny, you are a good dog!
You stayed.
That's what I wanted.

No, don't get up yet.
Tiny, stay! Don't come.

Oh, no, I forgot!
You don't know about *don't*.
You came when I said *don't come*.
I have to hug you for coming, or
you will be all mixed up.

Let's see if you can do it all again.
Tiny, *Come!*
Tiny, *Sit! Stay!*

That's great! You did it all!
How about a big hug?
We will do this over and over
again.

Now let's go for a walk.

Oh, Tiny, I said a walk.
Go slow, Tiny!

Slow down! Slow down!
Stop, Tiny, stop!
Oh, help!

I've Got a Dog

I've got a dog, as thin as a rail,
He's got fleas all over his tail;
Every time his tail goes flop,
The fleas on the bottom all run to
    the top.

—Anonymous

*How does a lighthouse help
boats on the river?
What makes the lighthouse sad?
What makes it happy again?*

The Little Red Lighthouse

by Hildegarde H. Swift

A little red lighthouse sat by a river.

Boats went up and down on the river.

At night, a light in the little red lighthouse came on.

The light helped the boats.

This light said, "Keep away!
Look out!
Rocks are here!"

The little red lighthouse was very,
very happy.

"The boats on the river need me,"
said the little red lighthouse.

One day many people came.
They were making something big.
It was near the little red lighthouse.

"What is this big, high thing?"
asked the little red lighthouse.

The people were making a bridge over the river.

The bridge was very big.

It was very high, too.

The little red lighthouse looked very, very little next to it.

A big light was put on top of the bridge.

One night, the light came on.

"That light is bigger than mine," said the little red lighthouse.

"No one will need me now."

The little red lighthouse became very sad.

"I will not put on my light," said the little red lighthouse.

Just then, the bridge called to
the little red lighthouse, "Little
red lighthouse, where is your
light?"

"Oh, my little light is not needed,"
the little red lighthouse said.
"Your light is bigger than mine."

The big bridge said, "My big light
is for planes and not for boats.

It is too high for boats to see.

Your light is for the boats on
the river.

Without your light the boats will not
see the rocks at night.

Here comes a tugboat.

Put on your light!"

The little red lighthouse said,
"Oh, my, that tugboat needs me.

I must put on my light."

The light went on.

Now the tugboat saw the rocks.

The little red lighthouse was needed
by the boats on the river.

The little red lighthouse became
very happy again.

What do the two owls in this story wish for? Who helps them? How?

Two Hoots and the King

by Helen Cresswell

Big Hoot and Little Hoot lived in the trees.

Big Hoot and Little Hoot were not wise owls.

They were two very silly owls.

Wise owls went to sleep in
the day.

Big Hoot and Little Hoot flew
when it was day.

"I would like to be wise," said
Big Hoot.

"So would I," said Little Hoot.
"I don't like being so silly, but
I can't help it."

Just then Big Hoot saw something
in a tree.

"Look over there!" Big Hoot said.
"What is that in the tree?"

"I see a yellow singing bird,"
said Little Hoot.
"It must be from the sun.
The sun is yellow, and so is this
yellow singing bird."

"The sun is the king of the day," said Big Hoot.

"So the yellow bird must be the king of the sun!

Let's ask the king of the sun to give us a wish."

"What can we wish for?" asked Little Hoot.

99

"Let's ask the king of the sun
to make us wise," said Big Hoot.

"Oh, yes!" said Little Hoot.
"It would be good to be wise.
I would say wise things all day
and all night."

"Not all day," said Big Hoot.
"When you are a wise owl,
you will sleep in the day."

Big Hoot and Little Hoot flew
to the yellow singing bird.

"Good day, king of the sun,"
said Big Hoot.

"We know you are the king of the
sun," said Little Hoot.
"You are yellow like the sun.
We can see that.
We would like you to give us
a wish."

"What wish can I give you?" asked
the yellow singing bird.

"Can you help us to be wise owls?"
asked Big Hoot.

"I can make you a little wiser
than you are now," said the yellow
singing bird.

"Good, good," said the two owls.

"I am not the king of the sun,"
said the yellow singing bird.
"I am a canary!
Now you are wiser than you were!"

Then the canary flew away.

"We were very silly owls," said
the two owls.
"Let's go to sleep."

And they did.

How Wise
Is an Owl

by Ilo Orleans

He sits on the branch,
    And he blinks his eyes,
And people say
    He is very wise!

Never a smile—
    Just a frown or a scowl—
That's all I see
    When I look at an owl.

He's awake at night,
    He sleeps by day,
He thinks it is wise
    To live that way.

*Faces can show the way
people feel.
What are some of the feelings
that faces can show?*

What Faces Can Show

by Leona H. Biz

A face can show many things.
Look at this clown's face.
Does this clown look happy or sad?
How do you think he feels?

Did you say that the clown feels sad?

Little Bear was resting.
"What do you want?" he asked.
"Why are you calling me?
I need my sleep."

"We want you to stop the rain again," they said.

"Why do you want the rain to stop?" Little Bear asked.

"This is the day for our parade.
Please, use your special umbrella
and make the rain stop."

"Oh, I just want to sleep," said
Little Bear.

"Oh, please," said the boys
and girls.
"Please use your umbrella."

"If I stop the rain, may I be in the parade, too?" asked Little Bear.

"Oh, yes," the boys and girls said.

Little Bear went out.
He put up his special umbrella.
Then the rain stopped.
The town had the parade.
Little Bear was in the parade.
Little Bear was very happy.

Relate Pictures to Text

Look at the picture.
Tell what it shows.

1. She ran all the way home.
2. She painted a picture.
3. He painted a picture.

1. It is a good day to read.
2. It is a good day for a walk.
3. It is a good day to ride bikes.

1. The girls are climbing the hill.
2. The girls are climbing a tree.
3. The girls are riding bikes.

Why does the boy in this play call "Wolf"?
What do the people of the town teach the boy?

The Boy Who Called Wolf

a fable from Aesop

These are the people who are needed for the play.

Narrator	**1st Person**
Boy	**2nd Person**
Sheep	**3rd Person**
Wolf	

Narrator: One day a boy sat on a hill.
He was looking after some sheep.
He needed to keep the sheep away from the wolf.
This boy did not like his work.

154

Boy: All day long, I look after the sheep.
All I see are sheep, sheep, sheep.

Sheep: Bah, bah, bah!
Day after day, all we see is this boy.

Boy: I don't see people.
I know what to do.
I'll play a trick.
I'll make people come to see me.

155

Narrator: So the boy played his trick.

Boy: Wolf, wolf! Help, help!
The wolf is after the sheep!
Help, help! Hurry, hurry!

Narrator: All of the people stopped working.
They ran up the hill to the boy.

1st Person: Where is the wolf?
Tell us and we will get it.

Boy: There was no wolf.
I needed to see some people.
I played a trick to get you
to come up the hill.

2nd Person: It isn't nice to play tricks.

Narrator: The people turned and
went down the hill.
The boy looked down at them.
Soon the people were working.
Then the boy played his
trick again.

Boy: Wolf, wolf! Hurry, hurry!
Help, help! Hurry, hurry!

Sheep: Bah, bah, bah!
We see a boy.
We don't see a wolf.

Narrator: The people stopped
working and ran back up the hill.

3rd Person: Where is the wolf?
Tell us and we will get it.

1st Person: Do you need help?

Boy: No, I was just playing a trick.

2nd Person: It is not nice to play
tricks on us.
We have work to do!
You must not play this trick again.

Narrator: The people turned and went away.

They went back down the hill.

Just then, the boy saw a wolf!

The wolf was coming nearer and nearer.

The wolf was after the sheep.

Sheep: Bah, bah, bah!

Hurry! Get us some help!

Boy: Help, help! Hurry, hurry!

It's true. It's true.

There is a wolf now.

Please help me!

This is no trick!

Narrator: The people did not come.
They were down the hill.
They were working.
The wolf was getting nearer
and nearer.

Wolf: You have so many sheep.
They are so nice.
I think I'll take some.

Boy: Help me! Help me!
It's true! The wolf is here!
Help! Hurry! Please hurry!

1st Person: Let's go and see what that boy is doing.
Who knows? It may be true.
There may be a wolf.

Narrator: The people ran back up the hill again.
The wolf saw the people, turned, and ran away.

Boy: Oh, thank you, thank you.
Thank you for helping me.
I will not play a trick on
you again.
From now on, I will be happy
just to look after the sheep.

Narrator: The boy now knows it is
not nice to play tricks on people.
He will not play a trick again.

A little mouse and his mother go for a walk.

How does the little mouse feel about the clouds he sees in the sky? Why?

Clouds

story and pictures by Arnold Lobel

A little mouse went for a walk with his mother.

They went to the top of a hill and looked at the sky.

"Look!" said Mother.
"We can see pictures in the clouds."
The little mouse and his mother
saw many pictures in the clouds.
They saw a castle . . .

a rabbit . . .

a mouse.

"I am going to pick flowers,"
said Mother.

"I will stay here and watch the
clouds," said the little mouse.

The little mouse saw a big cloud
in the sky.

It grew bigger and bigger.

The cloud became a cat.

The cat came nearer and nearer
to the little mouse.

"Help!" shouted the little mouse,
and he ran to his mother.

"There is a big cat in the sky!"
cried the little mouse.

"I am afraid!"

Mother looked up at the sky.
"Do not be afraid," she said.
"See, the cat has turned back
into a cloud again."

The little mouse saw that this was true, and he felt better.

He helped his mother pick flowers, but he did not look up at the sky for the rest of the afternoon.

Thinking About "Old Days, Old Ways"

In "Old Days, Old Ways," you read about some special days.

A boy and a girl needed a birthday present for their grandma.

A little bear used his special umbrella to help a town.

You also read some stories from the old days.

You learned about a boy who called wolf.

How did the boy almost trick himself?

What other days or old ways did you read about?

I hate it

when you get soap in my eyes.

What can be causing Persnickety Piggery

To put on that miserable pout?

Why is he squealing and snorting and scowling?

What is he shouting about?

I hate it

when you give him a bigger piece than me.

I should get the most because I like it the most.

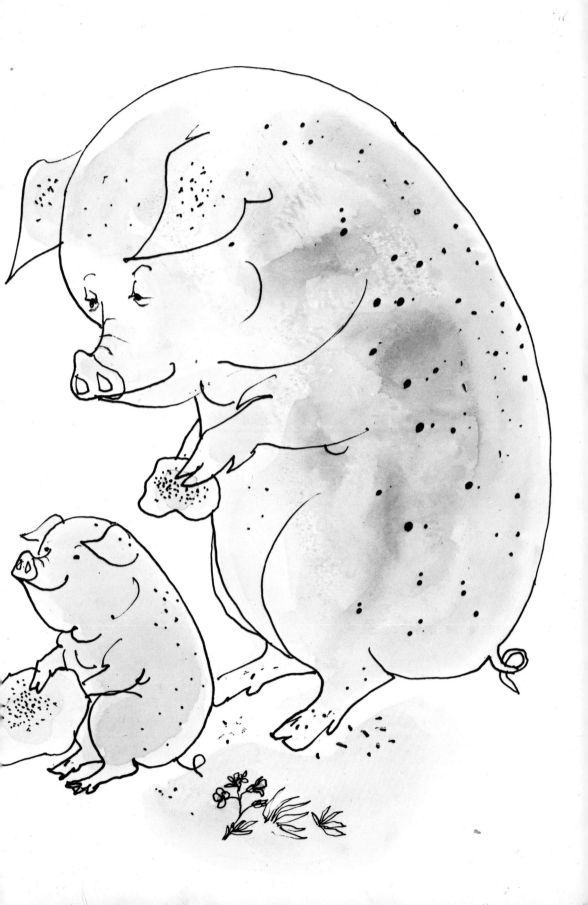

What is infuriating Terrible Turtle?

Why is he fussing so?

Why is he throwing a temper tantrum?

Where does he want to go?

I hate it

when you say I have to stay in.

And it's not even raining hard. I won't get wet. Honest.

What is exasperating Cathaleen Kangaroo

Making her glower and frown?

Why is she making disagreeable faces

Squinching her eyebrows down?

I hate it

when you make me stay still and not wiggle.

I *like* to flop around and put my feet up.

What is perturbing Olivia Otter?

Why is she making a row?

Why is she flipping and flapping

and floundering?

What is disturbing her now?

I hate it

when you make me stop playing

and I'm not through yet.

Why do I have to come in and
take a nap and nobody else has to.

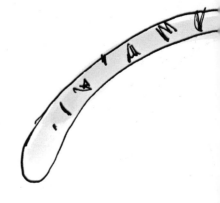

What is maddening Thomas Q. Tiger

Splitting the air with his yowls?

Why is he bawling bloodcurdling bellows?

Why is he growling growls?

I hate it

when you wash my face and rub too hard.

What can be pleasuring Henrietta Hippopotamus?

Why is she smirking so brightly?

What can be setting Henrietta to twirling

And whirling about so lightly?

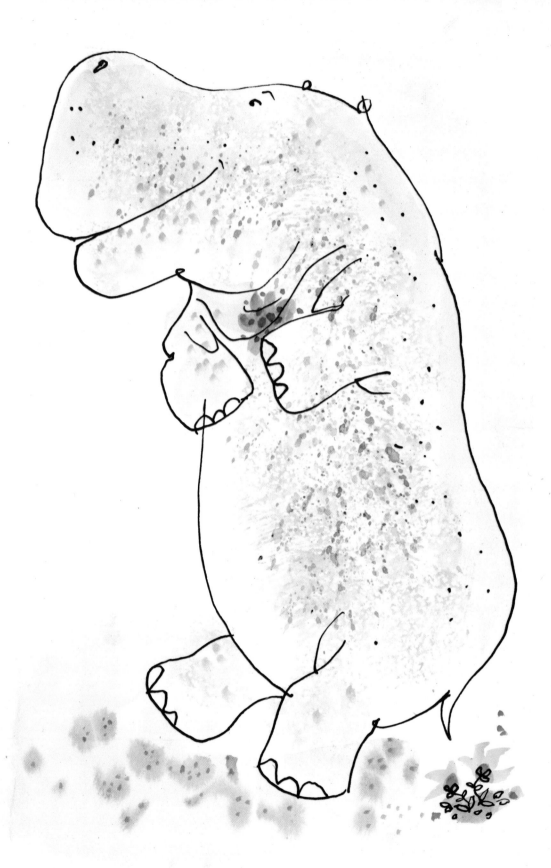

I love it

when you let me play in the mud.